Science and Technology

Aircraft

Andrew Solway

www.raintreepublishers.co.uk
Visit our website to find out more information about Raintree books.

To order:
☎ Phone 0845 6044371
🖨 Fax +44 (0) 1865 312263
💻 Email myorders@raintreepublishers.co.uk

Customers from outside the UK please telephone +44 1865 312262

Raintree is an imprint of Capstone Global Library Limited, a company incorporated in England and Wales having its registered office at 7 Pilgrim Street, London, EC4V 6LB – Registered company number: 6695582

Edited by Andrew Farrow, Adam Miller, and Diyan Leake
Designed by Victoria Allen
Original illustrations © Capstone Global Library Ltd 2011
Illustrated by Oxford Designers and Illustrators
Picture research by Elizabeth Alexander
Originated by Capstone Global Library Ltd
Printed and bound in China by CTPS

ISBN 978 1 406 22837 3 (hardback)
15 14 13 12 11
10 9 8 7 6 5 4 3 2 1

ISBN 978 1 406 22847 2 (paperback)
16 15 14 13 12
10 9 8 7 6 5 4 3 2 1

British Library Cataloguing in Publication Data
Solway, Andrew.
  Science and technology: aircraft. -- (Sci-hi)
  629.1'3334-dc22
A full catalogue record for this book is available from the British Library.

Acknowledgements
The author and publishers are grateful to the following for permission to reproduce copyright material: Alamy pp. **8** (© Stefan Hofecker), **10** (© imagebroker), **11** (© David Wall), **21** (© Keith Erskine), **26** (© Dan Lamont), **27** (© Emil Pozar), **35** (© Grapheast); Corbis pp. **14** (© Navy News Photo/Reuters), **15** (© Matthew Cavanaugh/epa), **17** (© Fabrice Coffrini/epa), **25** (© Logan Mock-Bunting/Aurora Photos), **29** (© Allen Fredrickson/Reuters), **36** (© Aero Graphics, Inc.); Getty Images pp. **18** (National Geographic/Volkmar K. Wentzel), **39** (Check Six); NASA pp. **6** (courtesy of the Kennedy Space Flight Center Public Affairs Office), **13** (Beasley); Photolibrary pp. **4** (Peter Hatter), **7** (Actionplus), **23** (Norbert Michalke), **31** (EPA/Fabrice Coffrini), **37** (Pres Select); Seymourpowell p. **41**; Shutterstock **contents page** bottom (© Germanskydiver), **contents page** top (© T.H.Klimmeck), pp. **5** (© T.H.Klimmeck), **9** (© Germanskydiver), **16** (© Carlos Caetano), **19** (© Charles Shapiro), **22** (© Philipe Ancheta), **24** (© chantal de bruijne), **all background and design features**; Vision Systems International, LLC p. **38**; www. jsf.mil/Lockheed Martin p. **30** (Damien A. Guarnieri).

Main cover photograph of a MIG-35 reproduced with permission of Corbis (© Sergei Chirikov /epa); inset cover photograph reproduced with permission of Getty (VCL/ Spencer Rowell).

The publisher would like to thank literary consultant Nancy Harris and content consultant Suzy Gazlay for their assistance in the preparation of this book.

Every effort has been made to contact copyright holders of material reproduced in this book. Any omissions will be rectified in subsequent printings if notice is given to the publisher.

Contents

How many passengers can this plane carry?

Find out on page 5!

What is terminal velocity?

Read page 9 to find out!

Some words are shown in bold, **like this**. These words are explained in the glossary. You will find important information and definitions underlined, <u>like this</u>.

FLY LIKE A BIRD

The sun is shining, but on the high hillside it is windy. At your feet is a grassy slope, then a sheer drop. You run a few steps and push on the bar you are holding. As you push, the hang-glider above you lifts. You are in the air! You soar out across a wide valley, shifting your weight to control your flight. You are as close as a human can get to being a bird.

In the past 100 years, humans have mastered the art of flight. Gliders can fly like eagles, spiralling upwards on a column of warm air. Helicopters can hover like hummingbirds. Airliners can fly thousands of kilometres, like an albatross. And military jets can dive and turn like a falcon.

Hang-gliders are the lightest of all aircraft. They can weigh as little as 24 kilograms (53 pounds).

Learning about aircraft

In this book you can learn some of the secrets of how aircraft fly. You can find out about **gravity**, which holds everything on the ground. You can also learn about air, which helps us overcome (be stronger than) gravity.

As well as the science of aircraft, we will look at the technology. What materials are used to make an aircraft strong but light? How have jet airliners cut down the fuel they use? Could aircraft of the future use **solar power** (power from the Sun)? Read on to find out.

The double-decked Airbus A380 can carry up to 853 passengers from New York to Hong Kong without refuelling.

FROM MIDGES TO GIANT JETS

- The **wingspan** (distance from the tip of one wing to the tip of the other) of a tiny midge is about 2 millimetres. A midge weighs half a microgram. (A microgram is one-millionth of a gram.)

- A hummingbird weighs about 6,000 times more than the midge. It has a wingspan of 9 centimetres (3½ inches).

- A wandering albatross is about 3,000 times heavier than the hummingbird. It has a wingspan of about 3 metres (10 feet).

- An Airbus A380 airliner weighs over 50,000 times more than a wandering albatross. Its wingspan is 80 metres (262 feet).

OVERCOMING GRAVITY

The hardest job that an aircraft has to do is to beat gravity. Gravity is a **force** (pull) of attraction found between all objects in the Universe. The more mass (weight) something has, the stronger the pull of its gravity. Earth is very heavy. It weighs about 6,000 billion billion tonnes. This means that the force of its gravity is strong. To get into the air, aircraft have to overcome the pull of Earth's gravity.

Blasting off

When a missile (weapon directed to strike something at a distance) blasts off from the ground, its powerful rocket engines push it away from Earth. This pushing force is **thrust**. But after a few minutes, the rocket fuel is exhausted. Once the engines stop, the force of gravity starts to pull the missile down to the ground again. Soon the missile is falling almost as fast as it flew upwards.

For a short time a rocket can overcome gravity, but when it runs out of fuel it will be pulled back down to Earth.

Without gravity to pull you down, bungee jumping would not work at all.

LOW GRAVITY

Planets, moons, and other objects in space that are lighter than Earth have less gravity. The Moon, for example, has only about one-sixth of the gravity of Earth. Astronauts in heavy spacesuits can make giant leaps that would be impossible on Earth. Saturn's moon Titan has a thick atmosphere (blanket of air). If astronauts ever reached Titan, they would be able to fly by "swimming" through the air.

A helping hand

A missile's rockets are so powerful that they can hurl it into space by brute force. However, missiles cost millions to build and can only be used once. Aircraft have to find other ways to beat gravity. So how do aircraft manage it? They get a helping hand from the air. You can find out more on the next page.

POWER OF AIR

As the big aircraft turns on the runway, you see that it has six engines. The huge wings seem to droop with their weight. The enormous plane rumbles down the runway. The nose lifts, and the Antonov An-225 has taken off.

A layer of air

The Antonov An-225 is the biggest aircraft in the world. It has a wingspan of over 88 metres (290 feet) and weighs around 600 tonnes. How can something so huge and heavy fly? The answer is that it makes use of the air. Earth is surrounded by a blanket of air, called the atmosphere. The air is a mixture of gases, mostly nitrogen and oxygen.

Air is very thin. Most of the time you hardly notice it. But in a strong wind, air can be very powerful. A hurricane, for example, can lift the roof off a house and carry cars into the air. Aircraft are able to make use of this power.

The huge Antonov An-225 needs six engines to get it into the air, and 32 wheels to cushion the impact on landing.

Skydivers join up in a formation as they fall at terminal velocity.

TERMINAL VELOCITY

Skydivers jump from a plane and then let themselves fall for a time before they open their parachutes. When they start falling, they go faster and faster as gravity pulls them downwards towards the ground. **Drag**, or **air resistance** (see page 11), starts to act as they pick up speed. Eventually, the skydivers reach a speed where the drag on their body matches the downward force of gravity. Then they fall at a constant speed. This speed is called **terminal** (final) **velocity**.

The terminal velocity of an object depends on its size and shape. Skydivers with their arms and legs spread can reach a terminal velocity of about 195 kilometres per hour (km/h), or 122 miles per hour (mph). Peregrine falcons can reach speeds of 322 km/h (200 mph) when they dive.

HOW TO FLY

A small aircraft lifts off from an airfield in a steep climb. At the top of the climb, it seems to stop in mid-air, then fall sideways. Smoke pours out of the back as it falls, twisting and spinning. But before it hits the ground, the aircraft pulls out of its dive. It swoops low over the runway, then flies upwards in a huge loop. It is the beginning of a stunt (performing) plane demonstration.

Getting lift

Unlike balloons, aircraft are heavier than air. Large heavy airliners take to the air every day because of their wings. <u>When an aircraft is moving, airflow over the wings produces an upwards force called **lift**</u>.

A parafoil is a collapsible "wing" that inflates when the wind blows. Parafoils are used for steerable kites like the one this kite-surfer is using.

How does lift work?

We can get an idea of what happens by looking at kites. If you make a kite, you have to be careful to tie the string in at least two places, so that the kite flies at a shallow angle to the wind. At an angle like this, the air flowing over the kite is turned downwards. This downwards airflow produces an opposite, upward force on the kite. This is lift.

FOUR FORCES

Four basic forces are at work on every aircraft flight. Lift pushes upwards, gravity (weight) pulls down, thrust (pages 30–31) pushes the aircraft forwards, and drag (pages 14–15) holds it back. For an aircraft to get moving, the thrust of the engines has to be strong enough to overcome drag and move it forwards. To get off the ground, the lift from the wings has to be more than the weight of the aircraft. In level flight, lift and weight are balanced, as are thrust and drag.

The Sukhoi SU-31 is a very popular aerobatics aircraft. Its wings are designed to make flying upside-down easier.

Wonderful wings

Unlike a kite, an aircraft does not need the wind to get into the air. It creates its own "wind" by moving forwards. The wings produce quite a lot of lift simply by being angled to the airflow.

An aircraft's wings are carefully shaped to produce more lift than a simple kite. The top surface bulges upwards, while the bottom is virtually flat. This shape is called an **airfoil**. In a wing with an airfoil shape, both the upper and lower surface work together to turn the airflow downwards. This produces more lift than if the wing was a flat sheet.

(a) An airfoil improves lift. (b) The amount of lift depends on the wing's angle to the airflow. (c) If the wing tilts too steeply, the airflow is no longer smooth, and the aircraft stalls.

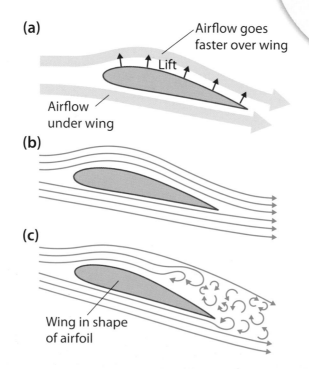

(a)

Airflow goes faster over wing

Lift

Airflow under wing

(b)

(c)

Wing in shape of airfoil

Spinning wings

Helicopters have **rotor** blades instead of wings. Each of these blades is shaped like a long, thin wing and is slightly angled to the airflow. When the helicopter starts up, the engine turns the rotor. As the rotor spins, it creates a "wind" over the blades. The angle of the blades, and their shape, produces lift as the air flows over them. <u>The faster the helicopter blades spin, the more lift is produced.</u>

WING SHAPE

Different kinds of aircraft have very different wing shapes. Aircraft such as gliders have very long wings. These give as much lift as possible at slow speeds. Aircraft that travel faster can get enough lift from shorter wings. The faster airflow over the wings produces more lift. Shorter wings are stronger, and allow the plane to be more manoeuvrable (easier to turn).

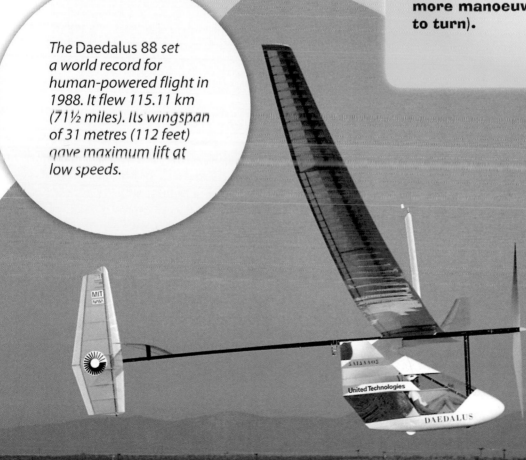

The Daedalus 88 *set a world record for human-powered flight in 1988. It flew 115.11 km (71½ miles). Its wingspan of 31 metres (112 feet) gave maximum lift at low speeds.*

IT'S A DRAG (AIR RESISTANCE)

When you walk down the street on a still day, you hardly notice the air around you. But if you are cycling into the wind, the air feels like a real barrier that you have to work against. This is how air resistance, or drag, works. At slow speeds, it is hardly noticeable, but <u>as speed increases, air resistance gets greater and greater</u>. Aircraft move fast, so for them air resistance is a big problem.

SUPERSONIC SHAPES

Some military jets travel at **supersonic** speeds. That means they travel faster than the **speed of sound** (around 332 metres, or 1,087 feet, per second). Supersonic planes have to be shaped in a way that will allow as little drag as possible. The nose of the aircraft is sharp rather than rounded, and the wings are swept back at a steep angle.

A "sonic boom cloud" forms for a few seconds as this F/A-18 Hornet breaks the sound barrier.

Slipping through the air

Imagine that a bus could move at the speed of a jet airliner. Air resistance would be so strong it would be like driving into a brick wall. But when aircraft travel at high speed, the air resistance is not quite so high. This is because they are shaped very differently from buses! The shape of an aircraft is designed to help it slip through the air. This is called **streamlining**. The whole aircraft has a smooth shape, and the front is tapered and rounded. This helps the air to move smoothly around the aircraft rather than slamming into it. If air flows smoothly over a vehicle, this greatly reduces drag.

This American Dynamics AD-150 aircraft is being tested in a wind tunnel. In a wind tunnel, the "wind" is produced by a large fan. Smoke trails show the movement of air around the aircraft. With a good aerodynamic shape, the air flows smoothly.

OCEAN STREAMLINING

The best place to see streamlining in the natural world is in the ocean. Water is much denser than air. It is hard to move through it at speed. Over millions of years, fish have gradually changed shape so they can move through the water more easily. Many have a tapered, rounded nose and a smooth, streamlined shape. Aircraft designers found that a similar shape helps aircraft move easily through the air.

SHIPS OF THE AIR

Balloons are the simplest type of aircraft. There are two main types of balloon – gas balloons and hot-air balloons.

Most gas balloons are filled with **helium**, which is a gas that is lighter than air. The earliest gas balloons used **hydrogen**, which is an even lighter gas. However, hydrogen can catch fire and explode. Helium is safer. It does not react with other substances and will not explode.

Hot-air balloons fly because of the difference in density between hot air and cool air. Warm air is less dense (heavy) than cooler air. So a balloon full of warm air is lighter than the same volume of cool air. This makes it float upwards.

DISPLACEMENT

A balloon or airship displaces (moves aside) a certain volume of air. The warm, less dense air inside it makes it weigh less than the volume of cool air it displaces. This makes it rise. This is what we mean when we say that a balloon is "lighter than air".

To keep a balloon in the air, a powerful gas burner is used to warm the air up when it cools down.

Round the world

In March 1999, a balloon took off from a small village in the Swiss Alps. This was no ordinary balloon. The silvery skin towered 55 metres (180 feet) above the ground. The enclosed cabin was designed to fly up to a height of 11,000 metres (37,000 feet). The balloon was the *Breitling Orbiter 3*. In the next 20 days it flew around the world, reaching speeds of 298 km/h (185 mph). It was the first balloon ever to make a round-the-world flight.

BRIGHT IDEA: A COMBINATION BALLOON

The top part of *Breitling Orbiter 3* was filled with helium gas. The helium made the whole balloon lighter. The hot-air part of the balloon made it possible to move higher and lower without wasting precious helium.

Breitling Orbiter 3 flew over the Swiss Alps during its round-the-world voyage.

AIRSHIPS

Balloons are simple, but they have a big disadvantage. In a balloon, you have to go more or less where the wind takes you. An airship is different. Airships have a streamlined "fish shape" that allows them to move more easily through the air. They also have engines, which allows them to steer the airship wherever they want.

WHO DID THAT? BALLOONING RECORD

US Air Force Captain Joseph W. Kittinger set a balloon record in 1960. He flew to a height of 31,300 metres (102,800 feet) – the highest ever for a human in a balloon. To get back down again, he jumped! He was in freefall (falling to the ground) for 4½ minutes. He reached a terminal velocity of 988 kilometres (614 miles) per hour before opening his parachute.

Bungee jumping from hot air balloons is another challenge that some people set themselves.

The *Hindenburg* disaster

For a short time in the 1930s, huge airships carried passengers around the world in luxury. The biggest of them, the *Hindenburg*, was longer than three Boeing 747 aeroplanes. All these early airships were filled with hydrogen gas. In 1937, disaster struck when the *Hindenburg* was landing in New Jersey, USA. The airship suddenly burst into flames and crashed to the ground in a ball of fire.

Modern airships

After the *Hindenburg* disaster, airships lost popularity. However, more recently, small airships filled with helium have begun to find new uses. The Coast Guard in the United States uses airships to patrol the coast. Airships are also popular for filming or taking pictures from the air. The US Army is currently developing airships that can be used as unmanned spy craft.

Airships are often used as giant advertising hoardings. The blue panel on the side of this airship is for an advertising message.

KEEPING CONTROL

Anyone who has played an arcade game will have used a computer joystick. You may have one on your home computer. You can use it to move a character, drive a car, hit a ball – or fly an aircraft.

Control surfaces

The **control column** on an aircraft works like a computer joystick. Move it forwards and the aircraft's nose tilts down in a dive. Pull it back and the nose lifts and the aircraft climbs. Push the joystick to the right and the aircraft tilts right. Push it to the left and the aircraft tilts left. The **rudder pedals** turn the aircraft right or left. The **throttle** (speed controller) controls the thrust from the engines. These are the main aircraft controls.

Taking the controls

The control column and rudder pedals control moveable flaps on the aircraft's wings and tail. The flaps on the wings are called ailerons. They control the aircraft's roll, or tilt. The flaps on the tail are called **elevators**. The pilot uses the elevators to climb or dive. The rudder is a large flap on the tailfin at the back of the plane. Turning the rudder turns the aircraft one way or another.

A BRIGHT IDEA: EARLY CONTROLS

The very first people to build and fly an aircraft were the Wright brothers in 1903. The brothers spent several years building and flying gliders. They also spent all this time learning how to control an aircraft in the air before they even started to design their first powered aeroplane.

TAKE-OFFS AND LANDINGS

At take-off, an aircraft needs more lift than it does in level flight. When it lands, an aircraft needs to be able to slow right down. This needs more lift, too. For both take-off and landing, modern airliners have large wing flaps that increase the area of the wing. This produces more drag, but gives more lift.

An airliner extends large flaps on its wings as it comes in to land. The flaps give the wings more lift to keep it flying at slow speeds and increase drag to slow down as it lands.

From wires to fly-by-wire

In early aircraft, aircraft controls were attached to wires which moved the aircraft flaps. However, as aircraft got bigger and faster, it became too difficult to move the flaps in this way. Most large aircraft used **hydraulic** controls. In a hydraulic system, the power of the pilot's movements is magnified by a liquid that is pumped through pipes. It is a bit like the power steering in a car.

Today, airliners and many military planes are controlled using **fly-by-wire**. This means that when the pilot moves the control column, it sends signals along wires to a set of flight computers. The flight computers then send signals to the flaps to move the aircraft.

A fly-by-wire system can do a lot more than just pass on the pilot's commands. On airliners, for example, the flight computers keep the aircraft flying straight and level if the pilot lets go of the controls. Features like this make a fly-by-wire plane easier and safer to fly.

The US Navy Blue Angels fly their F-18 Hornets wing to wing with pinpoint accuracy. The pilots are helped by modern fly-by-wire control systems.

Autopilots

An autopilot is a device that makes long-distance flights much easier for the flight crew. A modern, computer-controlled autopilot can fly an aircraft to its destination once it is in the air. Autopilots can even be used for take-offs and landings. In foggy or difficult conditions, the autopilot can land the plane more safely than a human pilot can.

UNSTABLE PLANES

Fly-by-wire systems have made it possible to build military planes that are almost too unstable for a human pilot to fly. But why do this? The answer is that if an aircraft is less stable, it is more agile (quick to turn). This is very important for combat (fighter) aircraft.

This is a view of the cockpit of an Airbus A330, which has fly-by-wire controls. There is a side-stick to control the aircraft rather than a large control column.

Controlling a helicopter

A helicopter does not have flaps like a plane. Instead, the main rotor does most of the flight control. Tilting the rotor allows the helicopter to go up, down, forwards, and backwards. It also allows the helicopter to hover.

The pitch (angle) of the rotor blades themselves can also be changed. When the blades are angled steeply, they give more lift for climbing. When the blades are at a shallow angle, they produce less drag, for forward flight. The blades can also change angle as they go round. This gives more lift on one side of the helicopter than on the other. By using the blades in this way, the helicopter can tilt.

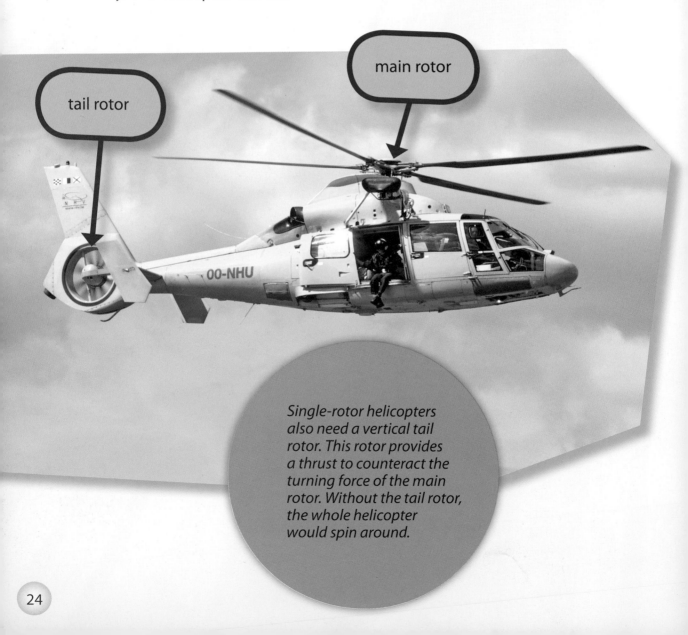

main rotor

tail rotor

OO-NHU

Single-rotor helicopters also need a vertical tail rotor. This rotor provides a thrust to counteract the turning force of the main rotor. Without the tail rotor, the whole helicopter would spin around.

Training pilots

Training pilots to fly aircraft is expensive, especially for large airliners and military planes. One way to speed up training is to use **flight simulators** (computer programs that are like flying a plane). Training in a full flight simulator is very similar to flying an actual aircraft. The cockpit is just like a real one. The whole cabin is on a platform that tilts and turns as the pilot moves the controls. And computer visuals show the view through the cockpit windows.

In flight simulators, pilots can safely practise flying in dangerous situations. These might be during a storm or when there is engine failure. They can also practise landing many times without having to take off again each time.

This pilot is demonstrating a flight simulator for a Cobra helicopter. The 3-D wraparound graphics show what the pilot would see on a real flight.

CUTTING DOWN WEIGHT

The Boeing 787 Dreamliner is at the cutting edge of airliner design. Parts of the body and wings are made in huge pieces. When a normal airliner is built, a metal framework is made first. This is then covered with thin aluminium panels. But the Dreamliner is made from materials called **composites**. Composites are the newest way to make airliners lighter (see pages 28 to 29).

The parts for the Boeing Dreamliner come from all over the world. The pieces are put together in this factory near Everett, Washington, USA.

Less weight, less fuel

It is important to make an aircraft as light as possible. <u>A heavier aircraft needs more **energy** (power) to get moving</u>. It also needs more lift to get off the ground. This means going faster to take off and to stay in the air.

The more energy an aircraft needs to fly, the more fuel it uses. Airliners fly thousands of kilometres each week, so cutting down on fuel use is important. Using less fuel also cuts down on pollution. Aircraft engines use fuels made from oil. These fuels produce the gas carbon dioxide when they burn. Increased carbon dioxide in the air is a cause of global warming (a warming of the Earth's climate). Using less fuel helps reduce global warming.

Lightweight metals

One way to build aircraft that weigh less is to use lightweight materials. A car or a lorry is made mainly of steel, which is strong, fairly cheap, and easy to shape. Most aircraft are made from aluminium instead of steel, because it is lighter.

Aluminium is more expensive to make than steel, and harder to shape and join. Engineers are always looking for new materials. Alloys (mixtures) of aluminium and lithium, for example, are about 10 per cent lighter than aluminium itself.

This view of an older aircraft shows how the "skin" is made of aluminium panels riveted onto the airframe beneath.

Composites

Composites are lightweight, tough materials that are being used more and more in aircraft building. <u>A composite is a material in which strong fibres of one material are mixed in another material</u>. Toughened plastics such as **glass-fibre** (very thin threads of glass embedded in a plastic called **resin**) and carbon-fibre are the most common composites. Airliners such as the Boeing 787 Dreamliner are about 50 per cent composites. Up to two-thirds of the materials in some military jets and helicopters are composites.

A REVOLUTIONARY COMPOSITE

During World War II (1939–45) the deHavilland Mosquito was built from an amazing composite material – wood! The aircraft's body was built from a wooden "sandwich". The inner and outer layers were plywood, with a filling of extra-light balsa wood. The lightweight body made the Mosquito faster than a Spitfire fighter.

How composites are made

Composites are made by laying down sheets of fibres in a frame, then injecting liquid plastic. The fibre layers can be arranged in different ways. For example, if all the fibres run the same way, the material will be very strong in one direction but much weaker in the other direction. If the fibre layers are criss-crossed, the material will be strong in all directions.

Single layer

Fibre

Plastic or resin

Strong in this direction

Multiple layers

Layers criss-cross

Strong in both directions

By using several layers, a composite material can be made strong in all directions.

LEARNING FROM BIRDS

Aircraft designers have learned a great deal by looking at how birds save weight. Birds have a very light, stiff skeleton that provides most of the support for the body and wings. Many aircraft also have a lightweight "skeleton" of metal struts (bars) covered by a thin metal "skin".

A bird's bones are extremely light because they are not solid. The inside of the bone is full of air spaces, like a honeycomb in a beehive. Some lightweight composites have a similar honeycomb structure.

White Knight Two is an experimental aircraft made almost entirely of composite materials.

Flight power

The aircraft on the runway looks like any other modern fighter plane. It starts its take-off run then suddenly swoops into the air. It has used hardly any of the runway. When it comes in to land again, the plane slows until it is hovering like a giant hawk. Then it sinks slowly to the ground.

This is a test flight of the F-35 Lightning II, the US Air Force's next **multi-role fighter**. It is able to take off very quickly and land vertically because of its vector thrust engine. <u>Vector thrust means the engine nozzles can be turned to point downwards for take-off and landing, or backwards for level flight</u>.

Jets and props

The F-35 Lightning II is powered by a jet engine. Jets are the main engines used in modern aircraft. However, jets were only developed in the 1940s. Before this, all aircraft used **internal combustion engines**. The fuel was burned inside these engines, in the same way it burns in petrol or diesel engines in cars.

The F-35B Lightning II has the most powerful engine ever fitted to a fighter aircraft.

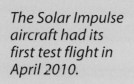
The Solar Impulse aircraft had its first test flight in April 2010.

Propellers

On some aircraft, the engine turns a **propeller**. A propeller is like a small version of a helicopter rotor. Each blade is shaped and angled to work like a wing. As the propeller spins, it produces "lift". However, because the propeller is mounted vertically, it moves the aircraft forwards rather than up.

BRIGHT IDEAS: SOLAR IMPULSE

In 2010 an aircraft flew non-stop for 24 hours using the power of the Sun. The Solar Impulse has the same wingspan as an Airbus 340 airliner. But the Airbus weighs about 200 times more! Solar Impulse's 12,000 solar cells powered the aircraft during the day. The cells stored enough electricity to keep the plane flying overnight. The Solar Impulse project is led by Bertrand Piccard, one of the two pilots of the *Breitling Orbiter 3* balloon (see page 17). He aims to fly the aircraft around the world in 2012.

How jets work

Jet engines (**turbojets**) produce a jet of hot gases that pushes the aircraft forwards. They get their power by burning fuel and air together. The air is drawn into the engine by large fans called **turbines**. Inside, the air and fuel mix together and burn. The hot, burned gases are allowed to escape in a high-speed jet. This jet provides the engine's thrust.

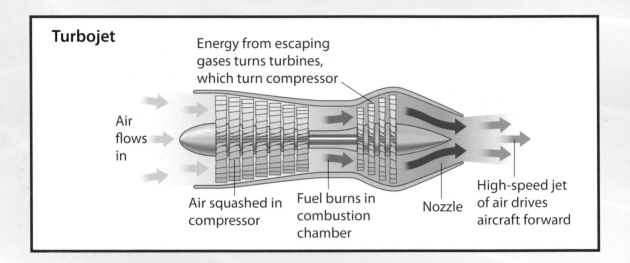

Turbojet

Energy from escaping gases turns turbines, which turn compressor

Air flows in

Air squashed in compressor

Fuel burns in combustion chamber

Nozzle

High-speed jet of air drives aircraft forward

Types of jet

In the earliest types of jet, all the air drawn into the engine was mixed with fuel and burned. In modern jet engines, some of the air goes around the main part of the engine rather than through it. This type of jet is called a **turbofan**.

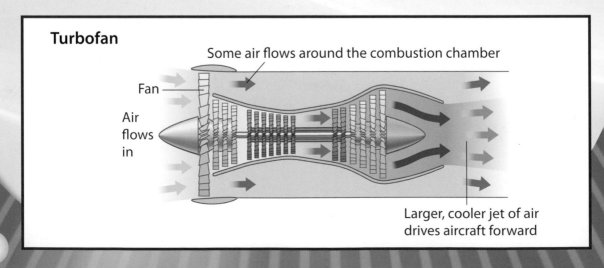

Turbofan

Some air flows around the combustion chamber

Fan

Air flows in

Larger, cooler jet of air drives aircraft forward

Fast military jets use a different kind of turbofan engine. More air is burned with fuel, and the jet coming out is fast and hot. This kind of engine is noisy and uses more fuel, but can move the aircraft much faster.

For an extra boost, military jets use an afterburner. This is a device that sprays fuel into the hot exhaust (escaping gas or vapour) as it leaves the engine. This produces even more power for the aircraft.

A mixed engine

For planes travelling at low speeds, propellers work much better than jet engines. Many small airliners and other smaller planes use a kind of engine called a **turboprop**. A turboprop works like a jet engine, producing a high-speed jet of air. However, the energy of this jet is used to turn a propeller.

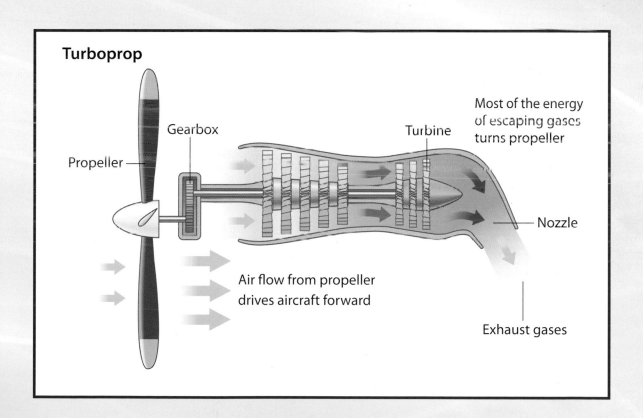

Turboprop

Propeller

Gearbox

Turbine

Most of the energy of escaping gases turns propeller

Nozzle

Air flow from propeller drives aircraft forward

Exhaust gases

RADAR

Early warning and control aircraft can detect (find) the movements of other aircraft and ships over an area of over 300,000 square kilometres (115,000 square miles). The most important part of their equipment is **radar.**

How radar works

If you throw a ball at a wall, it comes back to you and you can catch it. Radar works in a similar way. A radar transmitter sends out short pulses of **microwaves** (like the signals from a mobile phone) many times per second. These pulses bounce off surrounding objects and return to the radar detector, which "catches" them. From the echoes that come back to the detector, it is possible to build up a picture of the surroundings.

Microwaves reflect especially well from materials such as metals. This makes radar very good for detecting metal ships and aircraft.

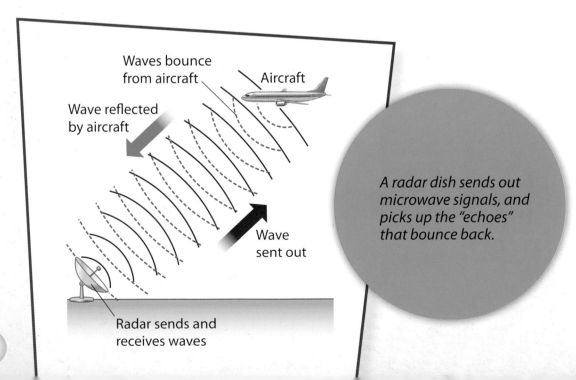

Waves bounce from aircraft

Aircraft

Wave reflected by aircraft

Wave sent out

Radar sends and receives waves

A radar dish sends out microwave signals, and picks up the "echoes" that bounce back.

Microwaves can travel a long way, so radar can detect objects many kilometres away. Microwaves can also pass through fog or rain, so radar works in bad weather. Radar systems can also "see" in the dark.

Using radar

Radar was originally used to detect enemy aircraft during World War II. It is still used this way. However, modern radar has many other uses. Pilots use radar to help them take off or land in the dark or in bad weather. Attack aircraft use radar to find their targets, and to give warning of enemy planes. At airports, air traffic controllers use radar to keep track of aircraft arriving and leaving.

FOOLING RADAR

In a battle, the two warring sides want to hide their aircraft from each other's radar. Many methods have been used to do this. Aircraft can drop small pieces of shiny plastic called chaff. The chaff reflects radar signals better than the aircraft itself, and hides its position. Another method is to "jam" the radar signal. This involves producing another radar signal that interferes with the original signal.

Without air traffic controllers using radar, there would be many collisions at airports.

Invisible aircraft

Radar is a very effective way to detect and defend against aircraft. To get round this, aircraft designers have tried to make military aircraft "invisible". These are called "stealth" aircraft. They have to do more than hide from radar. The heat from the engine exhausts has to be hidden from heat-seeking missiles. The aircraft also needs to fly quietly, and hide the radio or radar signals it sends out.

CLUMSY FLIERS

Early stealth aircraft were not as fast or as agile as ordinary fighters. The flying wing design was clumsy and the aircraft could not fly at supersonic speeds. However, newer stealth planes are supersonic. They also have improved computer control, which makes them as agile as other military aircraft.

The US Air Force F-117A Nighthawk was the first stealth aircraft to go into operation. F-117A aircraft were flying by 1983, but they were kept secret until 1988.

Stealth features

The design of a stealth aircraft starts with the overall shape. The wings and body are blended together in a "flying wing" design. This design is not seen so easily on radar. The first successful stealth aircraft, the F-117A, was very angular. The shape caused radar signals to scatter in all directions. However, more recent stealth aircraft have much smoother shapes.

Stealth planes are made mainly from composite material. These do not show up on radar as much as metal. They have a special surface coating. This makes them even less visible to radar. The engine exhausts are contained in tunnels lined with materials that absorb heat.

Many military aircraft carry weapons in weapon bays (racks beneath the body and wings). These weapons are very visible to radar, so in stealth aircraft they are hidden inside. But when a stealth aircraft drops bombs or fires a missile, it suddenly becomes visible on radar. One way to solve this problem is by having weapon bays that can open, fire the weapon, and close again within one second.

The F-22 Raptor is the US Air Force's most recent stealth aircraft. It has much smoother outlines and better performance than the F-117A.

AVIONICS

A rescue helicopter gets an urgent radio message. A climber is lying injured high in the hills. The pilot puts the climber's position into her **navigation system**. It shows her the route. The co-pilot says they must hurry because the weather radar shows there is a storm coming.

When they reach the search site, they find it is covered in trees. The co-pilot turns on a system that finds people by sensing their body heat. Suddenly a spot of bright colour shows on the display. It is the climber! They lift him to safety before the storm arrives.

Flying electronics

Avionics is short for <u>avi</u>ation elect<u>ronics</u>. Without avionics, the injured climber would not have been rescued. There would be no radio, no navigation system, no weather warning, no heat-sensing scanner, and no flight instruments.

Avionics allow the StrikeEye Helmet Mounted Display System to give pilots information directly on to the visor.

Fly-by-wires and avionics

Modern fly-by-wire aircraft (see page 22) rely heavily on avionics. Flight computers help to control the aircraft by constantly making small corrections. The electronic radar makes it possible to fly safely in bad weather. The electronic navigation system works out the aircraft's position and displays it on a map. An autopilot (see page 23) can fly the aircraft once it has been given the course. Even the flight instruments are electronic.

HEAD-UP DISPLAYS

A head-up display (HUD) shows important information directly in the pilot's line of sight. The latest head-up displays can produce a completely electronic version of the pilot's surroundings. They can show a clear view of the surroundings at night or in poor weather. They also display extra information such as the aircraft's flight path and any obstacles or dangers.

This is the head-up display in a Super Hercules KC-130J transport aircraft.

FUTURE TRENDS

In Croatia, a glider with a large propeller above the cockpit sits in a green field. The propeller starts to spin quietly. Then the plane taxis across the field and soars into the air.

At the same time, in the western United States a huge B-52 plane is flying at 15,000 metres (50,000 feet). Under one wing it carries what looks like a large white surfboard. The B-52 releases the "surfboard", which starts to fall. As it is released, the "surfboard's" engines roar into life. In fact it is an experimental aircraft. Suddenly, flames burst out of the back. It shoots away, leaving a white-hot trail.

Two views of the future

These two test aircraft are very different examples of how aircraft could develop in the future. The first is an electric-powered glider. It uses only a small amount of energy to get into the air. In the future, we will want aircraft that use less energy and do not harm the environment. These airliners may have engines that use electric power, or biofuels (fuel made from plant material). They may use a non-polluting fuel such as hydrogen. Future aircraft will probably be made from ultra-light materials, and may be solar-powered.

The X-51 Waverider

The second test aircraft mentioned above was the unmanned X-51 Waverider. This is designed to reach hypersonic speeds (more than five times the speed of sound). The X-51 Waverider is powered by a new kind of jet engine. It works at very high speeds and at high altitude (high in the air). Future spaceplanes will be able to fly into space without the need for huge rockets and throwaway fuel tanks.

In the future, there will probably be other kinds of aircraft, too. Giant solar-powered airships could carry cargo (goods) across the oceans. Tiny aircraft with flapping wings could be used as robot spy planes. Some of these aircraft already exist or are being developed. The future is just around the corner.

A London design company has developed an idea for airship "hotels" in the sky. The airships would be powered by a mixture of solar power and fuel cells ("batteries" powered by hydrogen).

FACT FILE

Fastest aircraft: In 2010, NASA's experimental hypersonic aircraft (even faster than supersonic), the X-43A, set a new world speed record for a jet-powered aircraft with a speed of about 11,200 km/h (7,000 mph). The X-43A flew without a pilot and was launched from under the wing of a B-52 aircraft.

Fastest piloted aircraft: In 1964, the X-15A reached a top speed of 7,274 km/h (4,520 mph). The piloted X-15A was powered by a rocket engine, and was launched from under the wing of a B-52 aircraft.

Fastest piloted jet: In 1976, an SR-71 Blackbird aircraft reached a speed of 3,530 km/h (2,193 mph). The Blackbird is the fastest-ever aircraft to take off from the ground under its own power.

Longest wingspan: The Hughes H-4 Hercules, nicknamed the "Spruce Goose", was an oversized heavy-lift seaplane built by aircraft manufacturer Howard Hughes. It had a wingspan of 97.5 metres (320 feet). The aircraft made its one and only flight, getting just a few metres above the water, in 1942.

Heaviest plane, heaviest lifter: The Antonov An-225 has a wingspan of over 88 metres (290 feet) and weighs 600 tonnes. In September 2001, the An-225 carried a record load of 253.82 tonnes, the largest load ever carried by an aircraft.

Biggest airliner: The Airbus A380 is almost 73 metres (239 feet) long. It has a wingspan of nearly 80 metres (27 feet) and has a maximum operating weight of 560,000 kilograms (1,234,600 pounds). Its first flight was in 2007.

Vital statistics

Name	Weight (kg)	Wingspan (metres)	Cruising speed (km/h)
midge	0.0005	0.002	10
dragonfly	0.001	0.018	15
hummingbird	0.003	0.09	29
house sparrow	0.029	0.23	31
common tern	0.12	0.83	28
black-headed gull	0.27	0.97	32
herring gull	0.94	1.40	42
pheasant	1.2	0.72	68
golden eagle	3.8	2.10	48
wandering albatross	8.9	3.00	70
Gossamer Albatross, a human-powered plane	94	29.00	18
Discus 12b hang glider	201	9.00	58
Cessna 150, able to carry 2 people	617	10.20	196
Sikorsky S-76 helicopter	4,400	13.00	232
de Havilland Twin Otter, a twin-engined light passenger plane	5,700	20.00	338
Harrier jump jet (able to take off and land vertically)	11,000	7.70	1,186 (maximum)
F-16 Falcon fighter/ bomber	16,000	9.50	2,124 (max.)
Airbus 320 airliner	73,500	34.00	840
B-2 Spirit bomber	168,000	53.00	765 (max.)
Boeing 777-200 airliner	265,000	61.00	905

Glossary

agile able to climb, dive, or change direction quickly

air resistance force which opposes the movement of objects through the air. Air resistance gets much greater as speed increases.

airfoil rounded, smooth shape of a wing. In cross-section it can be seen that the upper surface curves more than the lower one.

composite material in which strong fibres of one material are mixed in another material, usually a plastic resin

control column stick that can be moved forward, back, and from side to side, which controls the movement of an aircraft

drag force which acts to slow down a moving aircraft or other vehicle. Air resistance is the main part of drag in an aircraft.

elevators flaps on the aircraft's tail which make it climb or dive

energy ability to produce movement or activity, or to do work

flight simulator machine that produces the sights, sounds, and movements of a flying aircraft while remaining on the ground

fly-by-wire system in which computers help the pilot to fly an aircraft

force push or a pull that makes an object move, stop moving, stretch, squash, or change direction

glass-fibre very thin threads of glass embedded in a tough plastic resin

gravity attractive force between every object in the Universe

head-up display (HUD) instrument display that can be projected onto the glass of a windscreen or cockpit, or onto the visor of a helmet

helium very light gas, the second lightest gas of all

hydraulic something which uses liquid pumped through pipes to lift or move things

hydrogen the lightest of all gases

internal combustion engine engine in which the fuel is burned inside one or more containers within it

lift force which acts vertically upwards

microwave type of wave that is used, for example, in mobile phone and satellite TV communications, and in radar

multi-role fighter aircraft designed to be used both as a fighter and as a ground-attack aircraft

navigation system group of instruments which help an aircraft or other vehicle find its way from place to place

propeller large fan, usually having two or three blades, that can be used to provide the moving force for an aircraft or ship

radar *radio detection and ranging* – system which sends out pulses of microwaves and picks up the echoes. It can be used to detect distant objects, even in the fog or the dark.

resin thick liquid that sets to form a hard, glassy substance. Some resins are extracted from plants, while others are types of plastic.

rotor set of rotating blades. Helicopters have main rotors on top and may have a smaller one in the tail.

rudder pedal two pedals in an aircraft, which turn an aircraft right or left

solar power useful energy captured from sunlight

speed of sound speed at which sound travels. This is about 1,193 km/h (332 mph), but can vary with temperature and height above the ground.

streamlining shaping an object in such a way that it moves more easily through air or water

supersonic faster than the speed of sound

terminal velocity speed a falling object reaches when the downward force of gravity is balanced by the upward force of air resistance

throttle control that changes the engine speed of a vehicle – the accelerator

thrust pushing force that moves an aircraft or other vehicle

turbine engine part with blades that are driven by moving air

turbofan jet engine with a large fan at the front. It is quieter than a turbojet and uses less fuel.

turbojet jet engine that generates all its power from its exhaust

turboprop jet engine that uses the exhaust gases to spin a propeller

wingspan distance from the tip of one wing to the tip of the other

Find out more

Books

Danger Zone: Avoid Being a World War Two Pilot, Ian Graham and David Antram (Book House, 2010)

Danger Zone: Avoid Flying on the Hindenburg, Ian Graham and David Antram (Book House, 2008)

Fast! Jet Planes, Ian Graham (QED Publishing, 2010)

Jane's Aircraft Recognition Guide (Collins-Janes, 2007)

Science Secrets: Flight, Andrew Solway (Franklin Watts, 2011)

Smithsonian Q & A: Extreme Aircraft! Sarah L. Thomson (Collins, 2007)

Technology All Around Us: Aircraft, K. and A. Woodward (Franklin Watts, 2005).

Websites

Airbus A320 fly-by-wire demonstration
www.youtube.com/watch?v=WCc-R4xXZPU
Take a tour round the cabin of an Airbus A320 and learn how the pilot flies it.

First flight:
firstflight.open.ac.uk/index.html
This is a very easy-to-read, enjoyable guide to the science and history of flight.

Flight of the Jet Man
channel.nationalgeographic.com/episode/flight-of-the-jet-man-3757/wingsuit
Follow the story of Yves Rossy, the Swiss adventurer who flew across the English Channel in a jet-powered wing suit.

Milestones of flight
www.nasm.si.edu/exhibitions/gal100/gal100.html
Find out about some of the most important events in the history of flight through the US National Air and Space Museum's online exhibition.

Science fun with aeroplanes
www.ag.ohio-state.edu/~flight/homepage.html
Learn more about flight, try out controlling an aeroplane, and build
an experimental glider.

Flying the Wright Flyer
firstflight.open.ac.uk/takeoff01.html
At actual speed it is very tricky – try quarter speed first.

Topics to research

The pioneers of flight
Learn more about how the Wright Brothers became the first people to
build and fly a powered aeroplane. The Smithsonian Institution online
exhibition (http://www.nasm.si.edu/wrightbrothers/index_full.cfm)
is a good place to start your research.

Robot warplanes
Unmanned aircraft, flown by pilots from control centres on the ground,
are now being used to attack targets without risking pilots' lives. See
what you can find out about this new kind of warfare. Start by searching
for "UAV" (unmanned aerial vehicle).

What can we learn from birds?
Birds are superb fliers. How are their bodies adapted for flying? Can
science use ideas from birds to improve the aircraft of the future?
You can find some basic information on bird adaptations on the RSPB
website (http://www.rspb.org.uk/youth/learn/adaptation/flight/index.
asp). To learn more about how scientists are trying to copy bird flight,
do an internet search for "ornithopter".

Index